The Last Days and God's Priorities

The Last Days and God's Priorities

Lance Lambert

LANCE LAMBERT MINISTRIES
Richmond, VA

Copyright © 2018
Lance Lambert Ministries
Richmond, VA
USA
All rights reserved

ISBN 978-1-68389-087-4
www.lancelambert.org

Contents

Preface 7
1. Shaking in the Last Days 9
2. Four Priorities on the Heart of God 35

Unless otherwise indicated, Scripture quotations are from the American Standard Version 1901

Preface

The following messages were given in Toronto, Canada, in August, 1995. The spoken word has been transcribed and edited only for clarity.

1. Shaking in the Last Days

Luke 12:54–56
And he [Jesus] said to the multitudes also, When ye see a cloud rising in the west, straightway ye say, There cometh a shower; and so it cometh to pass. And when ye see a south wind blowing, ye say, There will be a scorching heat; and it cometh to pass. Ye hypocrites, ye know how to interpret the face of the earth and the heaven; but how is it that ye know not how to interpret this time?

Ephesians 5:6–21
Let no man deceive you with empty words: for because of these things cometh the wrath of God upon the sons of disobedience. Be not ye therefore partakers with them; for ye were once darkness, but are now light in the Lord: walk as children of light (for the fruit of the light is in all goodness and righteousness and truth), proving what is well-pleasing unto the Lord; and have no fellowship with the unfruitful

works of darkness, but rather even reprove them; for the things which are done by them in secret it is a shame even to speak of. But all things when they are reproved are made manifest by the light: for everything that is made manifest is light. Wherefore he saith, Awake, thou that sleepest, and arise from the dead, and Christ shall shine upon thee. Look therefore carefully how ye walk, not as unwise, but as wise; redeeming the time, because the days are evil. Wherefore be ye not foolish, but understand what the will of the Lord is. And be not drunken with wine, wherein is riot, but be filled with the Spirit; speaking one to another in psalms and hymns and spiritual songs, singing and making melody with your heart to the Lord; giving thanks always for all things in the name of our Lord Jesus Christ to God, even the Father; subjecting yourselves one to another in the fear of Christ.

Shall we pray?

Lord, we want to thank You that when we come together in the name of the Lord Jesus, it is never meant to be in vain, for You have made specific provision for the gathering together of Your people. Very simply, we want to stand by faith into all the provision that You have made through the finished work of our Lord Jesus. We stand by faith into that anointing of grace and power for the speaking of Your word, for the translating of Your word, and for the hearing of Your word. Father, let the word of

Christ enter in and dwell in us richly in all wisdom. Lord, work something in our lives that will be for eternity. We shall give You all the praise and all the glory. We ask this in the name of our Messiah, the Lord Jesus. Amen.

God is Shaking Everything

We are going to consider this little word in Ephesians 5:15–17: "Look therefore carefully how ye walk, not as unwise, but as wise; redeeming the time, because the days are evil. Wherefore be ye not foolish, but understand what the will of the Lord is."

Jesus was speaking to the multitudes when He said: "You can tell what kind of weather is coming from certain signs. You can tell the coming weather, but how is it you cannot understand the time in which you live?" (see Matthew 16:2–3). Of all the people in the world, true believers, those born of the Spirit of God, are meant to have an understanding of the times in which we live. That is why the apostle said: "Do not be foolish, but understand what the will of the Lord is" (see Ephesians 5:17). This is not only that we might know what the will of God is for ourselves individually, but we are to know what the will of the Lord is for His church and for His work in our generation.

When we look at the words of our Lord Jesus, it is perfectly clear that one of the characteristics of the last days is an enormous shaking. For instance, He says that men's hearts will faint for fear and for expectation of the things that are coming upon the face of the earth (see Luke 21:26). Why is this so? His word tells us that something will happen to the sea, to the moon, and to the sun. The powers of the heavens will be shaken. Of course, it is obvious if something happens in the sun, immediately, it will be reflected in the moon, and then the seasons and the tides of the earth will be affected.

In Haggai 2 we read: "For thus saith the Lord of hosts: Yet once, it is a little while, and I will shake the heavens, and the earth, and the sea, and the dry land; and I will shake all nations; and the [desire] of all nations shall come; and I will fill this house with glory, saith the Lord of hosts" (vv. 6–7).

Notice very specifically that the Lord said: "I will shake everything. I will shake all nations. I will shake the dry land, the sea, the earth, and the heavens. Then I the Lord will come."

Thus, one of the characteristics of the last period of world history will be a great and universal shaking of the moral and ethical standards of the nations—their social life, religious life, the whole fabric of human society in national life and international life. Everything that can be shaken will be shaken.

From Hebrews 12 we read this: "Whose voice then shook the earth: but now he hath promised, saying, Yet once more will I make to tremble not the earth only, but also the heaven. And this word, Yet once more, signifieth the removing of those things that are shaken, as of things that have been made, that those things which are not shaken may remain. Wherefore, receiving a kingdom that cannot be shaken, let us have grace, whereby we may offer service well-pleasing to God with reverence and awe: for our God is a consuming fire" (vv. 26–29).

It is the Lord who does the shaking. He may use Satan, ideologies or superpowers, and at the end, He may even use antichrist. Yet, it is always the Lord who is doing the shaking. He is not merely destructive, as if He is out to destroy everything;

but He is shaking what can be shaken so that which is unshakable may be made manifest.

The trouble with most of us is that we have so much that is shakable in our lives and we continue to hang on to these things. Our life is centered on the shakable, and the only way the Lord can shake us out of them and into the unshakable is by shaking everything. Then we suddenly discover there are a whole lot of things we thought were so important that are no longer important. Sometimes, people are very afraid if you talk about this shaking; but let me remind you that we will not be afraid if our treasure is in the right place. If our treasure is in the wrong place, we have everything to fear, but if our treasure is in the right place, we have no need to fear.

This shaking begins with the nations—with the earth. It goes into the heavenlies, which is the spiritual, and it will end with an actual, literal shaking of the universe. All the prophets agree with this—Isaiah, Joel, Amos, along with the Lord Jesus and the apostles. All of them speak about the physical heavens being shaken in the final stage, and nothing could be more truly designed to shake humanism to its foundation than shaking the sun, the moon, and the stars.

The last great ideology of mankind will be humanism. We have put a man on the moon which is the result of the exploring in space. We even have Russians and Americans meeting together in space which makes us very proud of what man is accomplishing. But if something were to happen to the sun, which would be immediately reflected in the moon and in turn affect the tides of the sea and the seasons, man would suddenly realize how fragile and small he is when these powers of the heavens are shaken.

That is exactly what the Lord Jesus said: "Men's hearts will faint for fear and for expectation of the things that are coming upon the face of the earth." It is quite possible that it will happen in our lifetime; for it seems that we are in the last era of world history.

We have already seen the recreation of the state of Israel and the re-unification of Jerusalem. We have seen two world wars in this century—twenty-two million were swept away in the first one and fifty-five million in the second. Since then, in China alone, if we take the figures of the International Red Cross, thirty-five million were liquidated between 1950 and 1965. Under Stalin's rule, altogether apart from two world wars, thirty-two million people were liquidated, and that is a very conservative estimate. I am not talking about the Babylonian period or the Roman period but the twentieth century in which you and I were born. It has been the bloodiest century in the long bloody story of mankind. God is shaking everything.

A few years after the remarkable Welsh Revival in 1903–04, there was a meeting in the small town of Llanellie in West Wales in a great old Presbyterian Chapel. The revival was still moving people, and the place was packed. Two old ladies were present in that meeting (long since gone to be with the Lord) who told me this story: "As the preacher was preaching, all of a sudden, he realized that nobody was listening to him. They had their eyes fixed on something over his head but, in spite of this, he continued preaching for a while. Then one of the elders in the front row beckoned for him to come down, and he pointed to something above his head. While the preacher had been speaking, a vision had appeared on the wall behind the pulpit. It was a scene of a lamb's head with huge human eyes, from which tears were running down like a river. That picture remained for over a half-hour, long enough that some people ran to get their neighbors to come and see. Obviously, the preacher never finished his message; instead, everyone fell on their knees, inquiring of God what it meant. They received understanding that a time of unbelievable trouble was coming on the face of the earth; but no one realized just how much trouble would come."

Everything continued, more or less, as it had for a thousand years, but in 1917 in World War I God shook the whole of human society. The Ottoman Empire, one of the great empires of world history, disappeared, along with the Austro-Hungarian Empire and the Czarist Empire. Then in 1911 the two-thousand-year Chinese Dynastic Empire disappeared. It was a period of unbelievable shaking.

World War II finished what was begun in World War I. In that war the British Empire, the French Empire, the Dutch Empire, the Portuguese Empire, and the Spanish Empire disappeared. God was continuing to shake, and ever since then, God has been shaking more and more. Seventy years to the very day that the Marxist covenant was signed in the Kremlin, that monolithic, invincible force that had overshadowed the whole of the twentieth century fell apart when God spoke the word. And we know that seventy years is a very interesting figure.

God is shaking everything. It is time to wake up; it is time to get ready; it is time to take heed. Let no one think they will escape if they are careless. We have no one to blame if we stand before the Lord with nothing because we have frittered away our lives and have centered on everything that is shakable and transient. We are receiving a kingdom that cannot be shaken.

The Lord Jesus put it this way when speaking to Peter: "Upon this rock, I will build My church; and the gates of hell shall not prevail against it." The Rock is unshakable. It is an unshakable kingdom because the King is unshakable.

Are we not stupid? We have the word of God, which is the revelation of His heart and mind. We have a salvation so full, so powerful, and so costly to God, by which He has brought us into union with Himself in Christ. The Holy Spirit has been given to us to lead us into the unsearchable riches of Christ that have been given to us; yet, we live like beggars. We are asleep—if not horizontal—then we are sleepwalking. How stupid we are!

Now can you understand why the Lord has to shake everything? It is the only way to reorient us. It is the only way He can readjust us so that we are able to center in what cannot be shaken.

The Last Days

We note these words in Matthew 24:44: "Therefore be ye also ready; for in an hour that ye think not the Son of man cometh."

How do we know that we are in the last days? Yes, there is a great shaking going on, but how do we know this shaking is taking place in the last days? Everyone seems to think that we are in the last days, but how can we truly know this? True believers have always believed that the Lord Jesus is coming and, indeed, there has hardly been a generation in the history of the church which has not believed their generation was going to see the coming of the Lord Jesus. The early church thought the Lord was coming, but He did not come. The Reformers, the Puritans, the Moravians, the Methodists, the early Brethren, the

Pentecostals—all thought the Lord was coming, but He did not come. The Lord's time frame is quite different from ours. Two thousand years ago, the Lord said, "I am coming quickly." We realize from this that the Lord has a different time frame from us. Nevertheless, the Lord will come, and when He comes, it will be suddenly and unexpectedly. If I understand what the Lord Jesus and the apostles have said again and again, it is not the world that will be caught out by the coming of the Lord but many Christians will be surprised.

We see from Matthew 24 that the disciples wanted to know about the coming of the Lord: "And as [Jesus] sat on the mount of Olives, the disciples came unto him privately, saying, Tell us, when shall these things be? and what shall be the sign of thy coming, and of the end of the world? And Jesus answered and said unto them, Take heed that no man lead you astray. For many shall come in my name, saying, I am the Christ; and shall lead many astray. And ye shall hear of wars and rumors of wars; see that ye be not troubled: for these things must needs come to pass; but the end is not yet. For nation shall rise against nation, and kingdom against kingdom; and there shall be famines and earthquakes in divers places. But all these things are the beginning of travail ... Now from the fig tree learn her parable: when her branch is now become tender, and putteth forth its leaves, ye know that the summer is nigh; even so ye also, when ye see all these things, know ye that he is nigh, even at the doors" (vv. 3–8, 32–33).

Then in Luke 21 we read these words: "For these are days of vengeance, that all things which are written may be fulfilled. Woe unto them that are with child and to them that give suck in those days! for there shall be great distress upon the land, and wrath unto this people. And they shall fall by the edge of the sword, and shall be led captive into all the nations: and Jerusalem shall be trodden down of the Gentiles, until the times of the Gentiles be fulfilled.

And there shall be signs in sun and moon and stars; and upon the earth distress of nations, in perplexity for the roaring of the sea and the billows; men fainting for fear, and for expectation of the things which are coming on the world: for the powers of the heavens shall be shaken. And then shall they see the Son of man coming in a cloud with power and great glory. But when these things begin to come to pass, look up, and lift up your heads; because your redemption draweth nigh.

And he spake to them a parable: Behold the fig tree, and all the trees: when they now shoot forth, ye see it and know of your own selves that the summer is now nigh. Even so ye also, when ye see these things coming to pass, know ye that the kingdom of God is nigh" (22–31).

Many people think that Jesus spoke this major discourse on His coming again—which we find in Matthew 24–25, Mark 13, and Luke 21—to the unsaved. However, it was not to the unsaved that it was given nor to the great multitude of lukewarm disciples, most of whom were going to fall away. It was not given to the seventy who went out in the name of the Lord Jesus and saw amazing healings and Satan falling out of heaven like lightning. It was not even given to the one hundred and twenty who were in the upper room on the day of Pentecost nor to the twelve apostles, the inner circle of the Lord Jesus. It was given to four of those apostles, the inner circle of the inner circle—Andrew, Peter, James, and John (see Mark 13:3). It was to those who were the closest to the Lord Jesus, the most understanding of the Lord Jesus, and the most discerning that Jesus spoke this discourse. When He said, "Take heed," it was to those apostles. When He said, "Watch and pray," it was to those four. When He said, "Take heed to yourselves," it was to those four. When He said, "Be ye also ready; for in an hour that ye think not the Son of man comes," it was to those four. If the Lord Jesus spoke this whole discourse concerning His coming again to those four disciples and His emphasis was on being ready, taking heed, the possibility of being caught out by the coming of the Lord, where does that leave you and me?

Everyone believes that we are in the last days—Islamic Fundamentalists, Orthodox Jews, and most real Christians; even the man on the street thinks we are in the last days. But how can we know this for sure?

Some people will say straightway: "The Lord Jesus gave signs which we find in the Scriptures. There will be wars and rumors of wars; nation will rise against nation, and kingdom against kingdom. There will be earthquakes, plague diseases, famines, and persecutions." But when has there ever been a single time since Jesus uttered these words that there has not been wars and rumors of wars, earthquakes, plague diseases, and famines? There has not been a single generation since the Lord Jesus uttered these words when all these signs have not been present. Of course, the world did not have telephones, televisions, fax machines, or satellites. When there was a famine in China, it would take months before anyone on this side of the world even knew about it. When there was a war on this side of the world, it took months, perhaps even a year, before they knew on the other side of the world. So the fact of the matter is that there have always been wars, rumors of wars, earthquakes, famines, and plague diseases; and there has nearly always been persecution.

Someone will say: "No, you are wrong. Jesus did not mean a war here and a war there, an earthquake here and a famine there. He meant world wars, and this is the first century we have known world wars." But I always ask the same question: How could any generation know that something worse was coming than what they were experiencing?

Suppose you had lived in the Thirty-Years' War that devastated a whole part of Europe. Would you not have said, "This is unbelievable"? Suppose you had been in the Hundred-Years' War. There was a war in Europe that lasted one hundred years, and thousands of people lost their lives. Out of it came plagues and famines, and at the same time, there was persecution. No wonder believers thought the Lord was coming.

Suppose you had lived in Europe in the great Black Death. Eighty-seven per cent of the population in the Mediterranean, Scandinavia, Europe, and Britain died. At the same time, there was war and persecution. Would you not have thought, "The Lord is coming"? How then can we really know we are in the last days?

It is very interesting how the Lord Jesus ended this discourse. In all three gospels where it is recorded, He ended it the same way. The question was this: "When will these things be [that is, the destruction of the temple and the exile of the Jewish people] and what shall be the sign of Your coming and the end of the age?" Jesus said, "There will be wars, rumors of wars, earthquakes, famines, plague diseases, but this is not the end; it is the beginning of the end." Then He spoke of persecution, and still He said:

"This is not the end; it is the beginning of travail, the first birth pangs of the coming kingdom of God." After this He spoke about the last stage—the Abomination of Desolation—an enormous period of tribulation that the Lord will have to cut short. After that He said, "Then shall the Son of man come in the heavens, and every eye shall see Him." Looking into the eyes of those four apostles, He summed it all up and said, "Learn the parable of the fig tree."

What is the parable of the fig tree? It is obviously important because we have it in Matthew 24:32–33, in Mark 13:28–29, and in Luke 21:29–31. The modern translation says this: "What is the lesson of the fig tree?" What did Jesus see that was so important?

Some people say the fig tree is just a picture of coming summer; that is, when the fig tree puts its leaves out, you know that summer is coming. This is possible; but the fact is that the fig tree is the last of the fruit trees in Israel to put out its leaves. When the leaves of the fig tree come out—which it often does in only twenty-four hours—it is only a matter of weeks before the long dry season begins. If He was giving a picture of coming summer, it would have been better to use the almond tree. If Jesus had said, "Learn the lesson of the almond tree," there would be no problem because, in the whole of the Bible, the almond tree is a picture of resurrection. It is the first fruit tree in Israel to flower. Hence, it is a herald of the coming summer. What then did Jesus mean?

The Fig Tree and All the Trees

Luke has a very interesting way of stating this parable. He is always giving us additional information. He said, "Behold the fig tree, and all the trees." It is as if Luke, as a doctor, was saying, "Be very careful; do not make a wrong diagnosis." We can observe two things here: the fig tree and all the trees. There is something that is common to both and something that has only to do with one tree. In other words, we have general signs and a particular sign. When the particular sign and the general signs come together, then you know you have passed into the last stage of world history. Jesus had spoken of the general signs, which are wars, rumors of wars, earthquakes, famines, plague diseases, and persecution; but here He says there is a particular tree that symbolizes something, and you must understand its significance.

The Fig Tree Symbolizes Israel

In the Old Testament, the fig tree signifies the promised land. There is a little phrase that comes at least three times in the Old Testament: "Every man shall sit under his own fig tree and vine" (see I Kings 4:25; Micah 4:4; Zechariah 3:10). This is not just a poetic phrase; but it means that every one of the children of Israel will have an allotment of the promised land large enough to grow a fig tree. The vine will grow up in the land, and the two will live together and fruit together, and he will sit under its shade. In other words, the fig tree is a symbol of the land, the actual soil of Israel. Jeremiah and Hosea tell us that the fig is also a picture of the nation. So we have both the land, the territory, and the nation.

In the parable of the fig tree in Luke 13:6–9, the Lord Jesus said that a certain man had a vineyard in which he had a fig tree. He came to this tree for three years looking for fruit and found nothing. He told the tenant farmer to cut the tree down because it was taking all the goodness out of the soil. However, the tenant farmer said that it should be given another year in which he would aerate and fertilize the ground; after which if it should bear fruit—good; if not, he would cut it down. The Pharisees and Sadducees knew exactly what Jesus was saying in this parable. He was speaking about the nation and its barrenness and His Messianic ministry of three years. It was not a year that was given to the Jewish people but a whole generation of forty years—from AD 30 to AD 70. In that forty years, the ground was truly aerated and fertilized, for it was the whole marvelous story of the early church. Yet Israel still did not believe and the tree was finally cut down.

This seems to me conclusive evidence that when Jesus spoke about the fig tree and all the trees, He spoke of the Jewish people as the validating sign. All the other signs are invalid unless that validating sign is present. But the moment the validating sign is present at the same time there are wars, rumors of war, earthquakes, famine, plague diseases, and persecution, then we will know that we have passed into the last days.

There is one more piece of evidence in the gospel of Mark, and for me it is the clearest evidence of all. On the day before Jesus said, "Learn the parable of the fig tree," something happened to a fig tree (see 11:12–14). Jesus used to spend every night in Bethany when He was in Jerusalem, and on this day, as they walked up the mount of Olives, they were in a place called Bethphage, which means "House of Unripe Figs." In other words, the figs never ripened for some reason in that particular spot. As Jesus came to the top of the mount of Olives near this place, to the amazement of the twelve apostles, He went over to a fig tree that hardly had any leaves and said, "I am hungry." Then they heard Him say, "You are cursed; no man will eat fruit from you henceforth for ever." The apostles must have thought: "Is He ill? Is there something wrong with Him? What has happened to Him? He knows all about the birds, all about the foxes, all about tilling, sowing, reaping, and harvesting; He must surely know that no fig tree in Jerusalem ever has figs in March." Poor little fig tree; it could not do what Jesus was looking for because no fig tree has ever produced ripe figs in March. What was Jesus doing?

First of all, had Mary and Martha not given Him a proper breakfast? Why were the other twelve not hungry? Now, we are given many explanations for this. The liberal theologians say, "Well, you know, Jesus was a man like us. When He became a man, He limited His knowledge; and when men are hungry, they are irritable. Jesus was hungry, so in a fit of irritation, He cursed the fig tree." I have had many old ladies come up to me and say they could not understand Jesus doing that to the poor fig tree. However, I cannot accept this explanation.

Then there are Bible-believing Christians who feel they must defend the Bible. They forget Charles Haddon Spurgeon's great words when he was asked to join a society for the defense of the Bible: "I will not join it under any circumstances. You do not have to defend a lion. Let it out of the cage, and it will defend itself."

In other words, let the word of God be the word of God, and it will defend itself. Only make sure you obey it. But there are Christians who rush to defend the Bible and say, "This fig tree is very special because where the leaves come out, there are little fruit brackets, and thus you can tell whether it is going to be fruitful." This does not explain why Jesus said He was hungry. You cannot eat fruit brackets!

In my estimation, Jesus was acting a parable. He went to that fig tree and made it a picture or an illustration. Later, when the Holy Spirit had come upon them, they remembered everything, just as Jesus had said, "The Holy Spirit will bring all things to your remembrance." They remembered that Jesus had gone from that fig tree into the temple, turned over the moneychangers' tables, let out the doves, and said, "My Father's house shall be called a house of prayer for all nations, but you have made it a den of thieves and robbers." The next morning of the evening that Jesus said to them: "Learn the parable of the fig tree," they passed by the fig tree and Peter said, "Master, look, the fig tree is dead, and it has died from the roots." Jesus said, "Have faith in God"—not at all meaning you can kill a fig tree by faith. This is what I believe Jesus was saying: "Where there is living faith, there is spiritual health. Where there is spiritual health, there is fruitfulness. Where there is fruitfulness, there is the blessing of God. Where there is unbelief or disbelief, there is corruption. Where there is corruption, there is barrenness, and barrenness brings the judgment of God." Jesus then had His last confrontation with all the different parties in the nation's establishment—the royal party, the Sadducees, the Pharisees—and it ended with the most severe message He ever gave (see Matthew 23).

Shaking in the Last Days

When Jesus went out of the temple through the gate Beautiful, the apostles said: "Look at that building! Look at the stones! They are so magnificent. For forty-three years, this temple has been in renovation." Then Jesus said: "Do you not see all these things? Not a stone will be left on another." Then they went down into the Kidron Valley and across the brook. Leaving eight of the apostles, probably, in the garden of Gethsemane, He took four of them and went up higher. They sat down, with the whole city spread out before them, and these four said, "When will this destruction of Jerusalem and of the temple take place, and what will be the sign of Your coming and the end of the age?" Looking into the eyes of those four apostles—all four of them Jews—Jesus began to speak and ended with the words: "Learn the parable of the fig tree."

The Fig Tree Back in Its Original Ground

What He was saying was this, and I am putting it in my words: "You are going to live to see this temple destroyed, this city destroyed, this state taken away. You will live to see the beginning of the exile of the Jewish people. It will seem as if there never was a fig tree in this soil. The judgment will be so complete you will hardly be able to imagine a tree was in this ground. But before I return, the fig tree will be back in its original ground, not as an antique, not as a fossil, but as a living tree with leaves coming out and the promise of fruit." In other words, the Jewish people will come back to the land.

It is a fact of history that ever since Jesus uttered these words nineteen hundred years ago, there has never been a Jewish state.

For just a few months, in the year 135–136 AD there was the rebellion of a false messiah called Bar Kokhba in Jerusalem. Apart from that, there has never been a Jewish state until May 14, 1948. Then the miracle happened. There was not a single military or economic expert that gave the Jews a chance in a million of surviving. Nobody thought the newborn Jewish state would survive even months. All hell was let loose. Two million young men in five armies came against it; and there were eighty thousand Jews able to meet them. Those armies were fully mobilized, fully equipped, fully trained, and three of them were trained by the British. Then the miracle happened; the two million fled and Israel was preserved. Since then, in forty-seven years, there have been six wars, of which four of them should have been the liquidation of this state—the War of Independence in 1947–1948, the June War of 1967, the Yom Kippur War of 1973, and the Gulf War of 1991. In all of these wars, little Israel has survived.

It is unbelievable. There is no other example in the whole world like it. All the prophets spoke of it. Even Moses spoke of it when he said, "You will be scattered to the ends of the earth, but the Lord will gather you. You will become a by-word among the nations. Everyone will despise you. You will wish when it is morning that it was night, and when it is night, you will wish it was morning. You will find no peace for your heart and nowhere to lay your head; but from the ends of the earth, the Lord will bring you back" (see Deuteronomy 28 and 30).

Jeremiah said, "As long as there is a sun and moon and stars, God will never stop the Jewish people from being a nation. When the sun stops, then the Jewish people will cease to be a nation" (see Jeremiah 31:36–37). In other words, they are a sign.

Jeremiah said, "Publish it in the nations and tell it in the isles afar off. He that scattered Israel will gather him, and keep him, as a shepherd does his flock" (see Jeremiah 31:10).

The Times of the Gentiles Fulfilled

There is no denying the fact that we have this sign, and it is a prophetic milestone. Furthermore, the Lord Jesus has deliberately confirmed this parable of the fig tree. In Luke 21:24, He said, "And they [the Jewish people] shall fall by the edge of the sword, and shall be led captive into all the nations: [This was fulfilled at the beginning of 70 AD] and Jerusalem shall be trodden down of the Gentiles, until the times of the Gentiles be fulfilled."

If you cannot accept the fig tree, at least understand that Jerusalem is the key to our understanding of God's economy. While Jerusalem was under non-Jewish government, the world was not in the end time, but the moment it passed under Jewish government, the world has passed into the last days. Jerusalem has been ruled from many other capitals—Cairo, Baghdad, Damascus, Constantinople, Rome, London, Amman. Jerusalem has never been the capital of anything in the last nineteen hundred years—except for the 11th century as the capital of the Crusades Kingdom—until June 7th, 1967. This is truly amazing! May 14, 1948 and June 7, 1967 are both prophetic milestones. The other amazing thing is that most Christians are asleep and have no idea what is happening.

Is there a Jewish state in this world? Of course there is, and we know all the fuss and controversy over it. Is Jerusalem the capital of that state? Yes, it most certainly is. From June 7, 1967 it has been reunited, and by an act of parliament it has been declared the eternal and indivisible capital of Israel. In fact, it is the status of Jerusalem that is the bottom line of all the so-called peace process; and in the end, that whole thing will unravel on the whole question of Jerusalem.

Is there a Jewish state? Yes! Is Jerusalem its capital? Yes! Have we had wars? We have had two world wars. In the first, twenty-two million were killed; in the second, fifty-five million were killed. Never before in history has there been a world war, but this century has seen two world wars, and at the very same time, there was the rise of Israel. In 1917, at the very point of World War I there was the Balfour Declaration. After seven hundred years of Islamic government, Jerusalem was liberated—not by the Jews—by General Allenby on December 9, 1917, which happened to be the first day of Hanukah. This is the Jewish festival of freedom which commemorates the liberation from the original antichrist. It is amazing!

At the end of World War II, Israel became a nation. Don't you think that is remarkable? Is there a Jewish state? Yes! Is Jerusalem its capital? Yes! Have there been wars? Yes; there have been two world wars and rumors of wars. We have lived in the rumor of another world war all the way until 1992. There have been wars and more wars—rumors of wars, and actual wars. Have there been earthquakes? Do I have to tell you? Are there plague diseases? We know there have been many. Has there been persecution? No other century has seen as many believers martyred as the twentieth century—not only in China, where probably a million believers were martyred, but in Russia and in Eastern Europe.

Moreover, no other century has seen so many Jews martyred—at least six million, and the figure is probably nearer eight million. Over fifty percent of the Jewish population died in World War II.

Sleepwalkers

We are in the last days, and the amazing thing is that most Christians are asleep. Now when you are asleep, you are not dead—you are horizontal. You do not walk, you do not run, and you do not fly. You breathe, your heart goes on beating, your brain goes on ticking, your blood goes on circulating, but you are asleep. So many Christians are asleep, and I am not talking about nominal Christians. They are not hearing the Lord; they are not alive to the Lord; they are not walking with the Lord; they are not running the race; they have no idea where we are in God's purpose.

Some Christians are not horizontal, but they are sleepwalkers and have a whole routine. They walk into the meeting asleep. They go to the same seat they always sit in, they stand at the right moment, they sit at the right moment, they even take the Lord's Table, but they are asleep. It is a sleepwalking routine. We walk, but we are asleep.

The apostle Paul said: "Let us not sleep as do the rest." But because many of us are asleep these words of the Lord Jesus fall on deaf ears. It is time to wake up. You will have no one to blame but yourself if the last events of world history catch you out. Our Lord Jesus said: "Learn the parable of the fig tree." Learn it; let it sink in; let it challenge you; let it grip you because we have very little time left.

Take Heed, Watch and Pray

The Lord has His eye on certain priorities which I will discuss. If we can understand them and adjust ourselves to the Lord so that we are moving with Him, then we will not be caught out by the coming of the Lord. So let us remember what Jesus said.

What do you think was the main emphasis of the Lord Jesus in His major discourse on His return? It was not the sequence of the events. He did speak of the sequence of the events, but that was not His emphasis. Nor was His emphasis on the details of those events. He spoke of the details, but that was not His emphasis. This was His emphasis: "Take heed that no man lead you astray. Take heed to yourselves. Take heed, I have told you all these things beforehand. Take heed; watch and pray." He did not say, "Pray and watch." He said, "Watch and pray." "Be ye also ready, for in an hour that you think not, the Son of Man comes."

People are always asking me: "Are we going to go before the tribulation, at the end of the tribulation, or in the midst of the tribulation?" I have a very definite view myself, but I have to say that in every interpretation of the rapture, we have problems. I believe it is by design. It is as if the Lord is saying, "You cannot live a careless life and then suddenly say, 'Now is the time; I must seek the Lord.'" On the other hand, if you want to kid yourself, you can go on kidding yourself.

Wake Up

Let me tell you the most remarkable thing the Lord Jesus ever said. It is not in the gospels; it is in the book of Revelation in the last chapter. He was speaking of His coming to the seven churches who were believers. He said: "Let him that is filthy become more filthy; and he that does unrighteousness, let him do unrighteousness still." In other words, if you are involved in dishonest business deals, go on; make more. Are you filthy? You can become even more filthy. "And he that is pure, let him become even more pure; and he that does righteousness, let him do even more. Behold, I come quickly; and my reward is with me" (see Revelation 22:11–12). This is amazing! It does not sound like the gospel. It is almost as if the Lord Jesus said: "If you want to wake up, wake up. If you want to get right, get right. If you want to continue on being lukewarm, go on. If you want to go on sleepwalking, sleepwalk. If you want to be horizontal, be horizontal. But I am coming. If you want to be ready, you need to wake up." May God speak to us and really reach us.

What I have said may make you feel a little uncomfortable, but let me say, you have no one but yourself to blame if you are not ready. If you do not get right with the Lord, if you do not decide that you are going to follow the Lord wholly, you have no one but yourself to blame if the coming of the Lord catches you out. May the Lord be gracious to us all. May He reach our hearts and touch us and, somehow, wake us up.

Shall we pray:

Lord, we need Your grace. Dear Lord, forgive us that so often we somehow pass milestones and we do not even know that we have gone past them. Wake us up. Somehow, get right into our hearts and make Your word live in our spirits. So often we say that if we had only been there at the exodus—but that whole generation died in the wilderness. Deliver us from Christian cynicism, from an evil heart of unbelief, and enable us, somehow, to wake up and follow You. We do not know how much time we have, but this we know: You can put into our lives everything we need to be changed into Your likeness, to serve You, and to be those to whom You can say, "Well done, good and faithful servant." Help us therefore, Lord, and don't let this word be lost. Write it deeply in our hearts. We ask it in the name of our Lord Jesus. Amen.

2. Four Priorities on the Heart of God

Luke 21:22–31
For these are days of vengeance, that all things which are written may be fulfilled. Woe unto them that are with child and to them that give suck in those days! for there shall be great distress upon the land, and wrath unto this people. And they [the Jewish people] shall fall by the edge of the sword, and shall be led captive into all the nations: and Jerusalem shall be trodden down of the Gentiles, until the times of the Gentiles be fulfilled. And there shall be signs in sun and moon and stars; and upon the earth distress of nations, in perplexity for the roaring of the sea and the billows; men fainting for fear, and for expectation of the things which are coming on the world: for the powers of the heavens shall be shaken. And then shall they see the Son of man coming in a cloud with power and great glory. But when these things begin to come to pass, look

up, and lift up your heads; because your redemption draweth nigh.

And he spake to them a parable: Behold the fig tree, and all the trees: when they now shoot forth, ye see it and know of your own selves that the summer is now nigh. Even so ye also, when ye see these things coming to pass, know ye that the kingdom of God is nigh.

Ephesians 5:15–17
Look therefore carefully how ye walk, not as unwise, but as wise; redeeming the time, because the days are evil. Wherefore be ye not foolish, but understand what the will of the Lord is.

Shall we pray:

Beloved Lord, we want to thank You as we come into Your presence that You have been in our midst. We have gathered unto You. And Lord, we truly can say we have been saved by Your grace. Now all we want to do is to recognize that without You we can do nothing. I can speak a lot of words, my brother can translate a lot of words, and we can hear a lot of words, but unless You are the anointing upon my speaking and my brother's translating and our hearing, there will be no eternal value. You have provided a specific anointing for this time, an anointing of grace and power. Into that anointing, by faith, we stand for the speaking, for the translating, and for the hearing. Fulfill Your design in our coming together, Lord, we pray, and we shall give You the praise and the glory. We ask this in the name of our Messiah, the Lord Jesus. Amen.

I want to consider four priorities that are on the heart of the Lord for this generation in the light of this shaking. In light of the fact that we are in the last era of world history, what are the Lord's priorities? First is the work of the gospel; second is the preparing of the bride; third is presenting every man perfect in Christ; fourth is the salvation of Israel. Let me tell you straightway that God will move heaven and earth to fulfill these priorities. His heart is centered on these matters, and if you want to reach the end of the Lord, all the grace of the Lord Jesus and all the power of the Holy Spirit are made available to you. You and I will have no excuse.

The Work of the Gospel

In Matthew 24:14 it says, "And this gospel of the kingdom shall be preached in the whole world for a testimony unto all the nations; and then shall the end come."

Some people immediately say to me that this is not the gospel of salvation but the gospel of the kingdom, as if the gospel of God's saving grace and the gospel of the kingdom are two different things. But the gospel that the Lord Jesus and the apostles preached was the gospel of the kingdom. In other words, it was the declaration that God is absolutely sovereign, that nothing can frustrate God, that God works all things according to the counsel of His own will, and that God commands men everywhere to repent because He has given us a Savior in the Person of our Lord Jesus. This is the gospel of the kingdom. It is to be preached in all the world for a testimony to all nations, and only then shall the end come. The record we have in Mark 13:10 says, "And the gospel must first be preached unto all the nations."

How much heart do you have for the work of the gospel? I do not know what it is about Christians, but it is very interesting to me that people who center around the deeper things often have very little time for evangelism. It is as if when we have seen what the church is and what God's eternal purpose is, we are somehow excused from preaching the gospel. "We must center upon the building of the church." There comes a kind of implication or a kind of inference that says: "That is merely gospel work! Kindergarten! It is elementary. We left that behind years ago." How can any company of God's children walk with the Lord, who died to save the world, and not have any burden for this work? There is something terribly wrong. How can anyone walk in step with their Lord, who died for the world, and have no burden for the unsaved men and women in their office or for their unsaved relatives? It cannot be.

I go from group to group, from company to company, and as far as I can see, most people are pretty comfortable. They have a reasonably good standard of life, especially in North America and in Western Europe. Very rarely do I ever find anyone who has a burden for the front line. I travel all over the world, and I see servants of God in the most extraordinary places—sometimes in the rain forests, sometimes in the mountains, sometimes far, far away from the centers of civilization. These are faithful servants of God, facing the powers of darkness with no one behind them, no one praying for them, no one caring for them. No wonder the first shall be last and the last shall be first.

It says in Joel, and it is quoted again in Acts: "The sun shall be turned into darkness, and the moon into blood, before the great and terrible day of the Lord cometh. And it shall come to pass, that whosoever shall call on the name of the Lord shall be delivered; for in mount Zion and in Jerusalem there shall be those that escape, as the Lord hath said" (Joel 2:31–32).

I understand this prophecy to mean that right up to the actual coming of the Lord people will be saved. It says it again in Joel 3:14: "Multitudes, multitudes in the valley of decision!" In other words, when everything is being shaken, when there are enormous divine judgments on the nations, yet there shall be those that will be saved. Even in the book of Revelation, it speaks of a great innumerable company coming out of the tribulation, having washed their robes in the blood of the Lamb.

"Whosoever shall call upon the name of the Lord shall be saved. How then shall they call on him in whom they have not believed? and how shall they believe in him whom they have not heard? and how shall they hear without a preacher? and how shall they preach, except they be sent? even as it is written, How beautiful are the feet of them that bring glad tidings of good things!" (Romans 10:13–15)

How can these people call upon the name of the Lord if they have never heard what the name of the Lord is? How can they call upon the name of someone they do not know what He has done, unless someone preaches? "For faith comes by hearing, and hearing by the word of Christ" (see Romans 10:17).

But how will they have the word of Christ unless there is someone who goes?

I was born in Britain. How did a British church ever come into being if there were not some people who laid down their lives to preach the gospel there when there were no Christians? And what about China? How in the world did the gospel ever get to China? Did people sit on the other side of the earth and say, "Oh well, God will do it. Maybe it is not God's purpose to save the Chinese. Maybe He does not like the Chinese. Maybe we should forget the Chinese and just sit at home. We will sit in Britain; we will sit in Norway; we will sit in Sweden; we will sit in Canada." No; whatever faults they had, God called them, and they went; they laid down their lives. Today, the greatest ethnic group of believers in the world is in mainland China, and it all came from the preaching of the gospel.

We know that not all of us are called to the far-flung parts of the earth; but why are we not behind servants of God who are called? In our local assemblies are there not servants of God seeking to reach the drug addicts, the alcoholics, the hopeless? Why do we despise it, as if this is kindergarten or something we have left behind long ago? Oftentimes, this is the way we think: "We are far too spiritual to be involved in things like that." What is wrong with us? Who was the most spiritual person who ever walked the earth? Of course, it was the Lord Jesus—and He was found among the publicans and sinners. Where are publicans and sinners? Some Christians are so separated from the world they never see a publican or sinner. They are on their way to heaven, and all they can do is sing hymns and read the Bible. They have no touch with publicans and sinners, but this is a priority with

God. This gospel must be preached first in all the earth before the Lord comes.

This is a priority. It is not something from which you can be excused; it is a priority. You are accountable to God for this priority. One day, the Lord will want an account from you. Even if you were not called to go, did you have a heart for it? Did you pray? Did you support? Did you help financially? We are accountable. May God give us grace.

The Bride

The second priority is the bride. Isn't it amazing that the Bible begins with a wedding, ends with a wedding, and in the middle of the Bible, there is another wedding (see Genesis 2, Revelation 21, and the little Song of Solomon)? Do you not think that is significant? Do you not think it is remarkable that when Jesus began His Messianic ministry, the first sign He ever performed was at a wedding? When John the Baptist spoke of his ministry, he said, "I am the best man of the Bridegroom." When Paul spoke of the churches he had founded, he said, "I am seeking to present you as a virgin bride to the Bridegroom." What a tremendous thing this is!

In Revelation 19, in the midst of all the terrible visions of beasts coming up out of the sea, beasts coming up out of the earth, antichrist, demonized human beings, judgment on Babylon, and persecution, suddenly, we hear this cry: "Hallelujah: for the Lord our God, the Almighty reigneth. Let us rejoice and be exceeding glad, and let us give the glory unto him: for the marriage of the Lamb is come, and his [bride] hath made herself ready" (Revelation 19:6b–7). This is something unbelievable.

In the second chapter of the Bible, there is a wedding in time. It is between two human beings—Adam and Eve—and it is till death parts. At the end of the Bible, precisely corresponding to Genesis 2, there is another wedding between the Lamb and the wife of the Lamb—it is forever. The whole Bible is an amazing story. It is no coincidence that there is a divine order even in the books of the Bible.

We see this matter introduced in Genesis 2. Adam was on his own, and it says, "And there was no help meet found for him." But then the Lord called all the animals and said to Adam, "Adam, name them." I used to think how strange this was. When I was twelve years of age, I had never read the Bible, so when I first read it, I was very amazed. I wondered why the Lord told Adam to name the animals. God created them, why didn't He name them? He could have said, "Adam, this is an el-e-phant."

Adam would have said, "Elephant, that is right."

"Adam, this is a giraffe."

"Yes," Adam would have said, "a giraffe."

"Now this is a hip-po-pot-amus," and the hippopotamus lumbered by.

What was the Lord doing? The Lord was saying, "Adam, what are you going to call this?"

Adam looked at this great creature with its long trunk, and he said, "Elephant."

The Lord said, "Elephant."

Then came the giraffe, so elegant with its long neck. Maybe it turned its neck around and looked at Adam, and Adam said, "Giraffe."

The Lord said, "Giraffe."

Then came a hippo. He opened his mouth wide, and Adam looked in and said, "Hippopotamus."

"Yes," said the Lord, "Hippopotamus."

What was the Lord trying to do? We know that Adam was without sin, but he was not complete. God was trying to bring him to a place of realizing his loneliness. "Can you live with the elephant? a giraffe? a hippopotamus?" Then came the orangutan. Orangutan in Bahasa Malay means "man of the forest." Adam may have thought to himself: "Can I? Could I live with this? Could I share my life with this? No; this is an orangutan." The orangutan left, and then it says, "There was no help meet found for Adam." God put him to sleep, opened his side, took flesh and bone, and created woman. When Adam woke up, he did not say, "Oh, this is woman; good-bye." He said, "I am man; this is woman." In Hebrew, it is ish, ishshah. The Scripture says, "For this cause a man shall leave his father and mother and shall be joined to his wife, and the two shall become one flesh."

Now, let us take a look at the cross. After Jesus finished the work of our salvation, after He cried that great triumphant cry, "It is finished!" then a soldier came to Him with a spear and pierced Jesus' side, and out came blood and water. Then John said: "I saw it, and my witness is true" (see John 19:34–35)—as if it is very, very important.

Some say, "This has to do with salvation." Of course, it has to do with salvation, but actually our salvation was already won.

Four Priorities on the Heart of God 43

What is it? It is the second Man. God put Him to sleep, opened His side, took blood and water and created the bride. Later, John wrote in 1 John 5: "There are three that bear witness—the Spirit, the water, and the blood" (see v. 8). The Holy Spirit is taking the blood and the water and creating the church.

In the heart of the Bible there is a little book called Song of Songs, and this is another wedding which is in the very heart of the Bible. It was a vision given to Solomon, revealing the love of God for His own. All I want to get over to you is that you have a wedding at the beginning of the Bible, a wedding at the end of the Bible, and a wedding in the middle of the Bible.

In the little book of Ecclesiastes, we cannot but notice that all it says is: "Vanity, vanity, all is vanity. Emptiness, emptiness, all is emptiness. Uselessness, uselessness, all is uselessness." When we come to the Song of Solomon, it is purpose, purpose, all is purposeful. In other words, God has a purpose. If you and I do not come into His purpose, everything is empty, vain, and useless. But after we have been saved by the grace of God and are allowing the Lord to train us, instruct us, and bring us to full maturity, then everything is precious. Every circumstance, every problem, and every difficulty are all turned to good account.

There are four gospels, three of which are histories—Matthew, Mark, and Luke. But John is an interpretation, and it is built on eight signs and eight declarations. We know that the first miracle that Jesus ever performed was at a wedding, and it was turning water into wine—not wine into water, as some Christians would like to say. Jesus began His Messianic ministry with a sign, and it was at a wedding.

John the Baptist described himself as the best man of the Bridegroom. The apostle Paul said, "Christ also loved the church and gave Himself up for it, that He might present to Himself a glorious church without spot or wrinkle." Then he said, "For this cause a man shall leave his father and mother, and the two shall become one. This mystery is great: but I speak of Christ and the church" (see Ephesians 5:29–32). Wherever we look, it is the same thing.

At the end of the Bible, that bride is produced out of only three materials—gold, precious stones, and pearl. That bride is also called a capital city—the new Jerusalem, the heavenly city. Now I find this quite extraordinary. Here are two quite different ideas brought together—a bride and a capital city. Nobody has ever introduced his wife to me: "This is my capital city." No one would even think of it. Nobody would ever think of calling his bride or his wife a capital city. But when the Bible finishes, it is with a bride. The bride is a capital city, and the capital city is a bride, as if the Lord is saying, "I want those who have grown up, those who have come to full knowledge, those who can reign with Me, those who can administer the will of God." A capital city is where all the government is centered and every issue is settled. It is as if the Lord is saying, "I do not want an eternal civil service nor a bureaucracy; I want a companion who will remain in a quality of love called first love."

There is among some Christians an idea that we will reign willy-nilly. We may never have grown down here. We may still be little babies twenty or forty years after we have been saved, but somehow we are going to reign with Christ. May the Lord help us. Some people cannot even govern their kitchen nor their pet, the family dog. There are some who have this idea that as long as they are beautiful—like a kind of spiritual Marilyn Monroe—with beautiful complexion, beautiful eyelashes, beautiful eyes, beautiful hair, beautiful hands, beautiful feet, beautiful figure, and nothing between each ear, that is all the Lord wants. He wants someone who will sit with Him on the throne and people will be able to say: "Isn't she beautiful?" But that is not what the Lord wants. The Lord wants someone who has followed Him, who has been totally committed to Him, and who has entered into the kingdom through many tribulations. This means that we have to grow up.

We must remain awake—not sleepwalking through our life here with one another. But what are our meetings? So often, they are a sleepwalking routine. We can go through the whole thing asleep. We come in, we sit down, we bow our heads, we lift up our heads. Someone gives us a hymn, and we sing it. Then we close it. We sing another hymn, and we close it. Anyone can go through the routine. Even the Lord's Table is a routine for many. We could come in asleep, find our place, sit down, and never wake up once. We could listen to one whole hour of brother Lambert and be asleep. It goes in one ear and out the other. It tickles our brain like a dream. It comes in and goes out. They may be wonderful truths, but as fast as they come in, just as fast it is gone. When someone asks us what brother Lambert talked about, we have to think and think: "I think it was something about the coming of the Lord." It is a sleepwalking routine. We can go through the whole of our life like this.

What does it mean to be the church? It means we belong to the Lord Jesus and to one another. We love the Lord Jesus; we love one another. Our greatest problem is relationships—how to stay together. Most of the time we get so upset with one another that there are people we will not talk to. "If so and so is sitting here, I am going to sit over there." But then we have the Lord's Table and pretend we are all one. What does it mean to be the bride? It comes down to very practical relationships.

Let me put it this way. Jacob was the biggest swindler in the Middle East. He was very clever, and in many ways, very spiritual; but he was a swindler. Yet, he did not know it. He was doing what came naturally. Of course, he loved God. He loved the birthright and he loved the blessing, but he was a twister. His very name in Hebrew means "twister." He could not help it. So God sent him to the second greatest swindler in the Middle East—Uncle Laban. Uncle Laban and Nephew Jacob swindled each other for twenty years until finally Jacob woke up. He saw himself in his Uncle Laban, in his wife Leah, and in his beloved Rachel. Only then was he ready for a life-transforming experience. The angel of the Lord never could have wrestled with Jacob earlier than that point. It was a divine appointment. This is the church. The church is Beth-el, "house of God." When Jacob started out on his journey, he put his head on a stone, and he called it Beth-el, "house of God." When he came back, he anointed the same pillow. His whole experience was bounded by the house of God.

This is a priority—and a very important one. Where do you stand in relation to the bride? Are you prepared to follow the

Lord the whole way? May the Lord help us, and may He reach our hearts.

Presenting Every Man Perfect in Christ

The third priority in God's priorities is you, personally, and we read of this in Colossians 1:27–28: "To whom God was pleased to make known what is the riches of the glory of this mystery among the Gentiles, which is Christ in you, the hope of glory: whom we proclaim, admonishing every man and teaching every man in all wisdom, that we may present every man perfect in Christ."

What does it mean to present every man perfect in Christ? You may be a child of God; you may have been saved by the grace of God; you may have been born of the Spirit of God; but you are not full-grown. You have to go on to full-growth. There is nothing instant with God. We have instant coffee, instant cream, instant pies, instant mixes, instant everything. We all want to have instant salvation, instant holiness, instant full-growth, instant everything, but growth is growth.

Many years ago, believe it or not, I was the size of a baby, amazing as that may seem to you. My mother said I was so ugly that when she first saw me, she wept. She said to my grandmother, "I am sure there has been a mix-up with the baby." I was just a small baby, and now I am a full-grown man. How did it happen?

"Well," you say, "you were sent to the university."

"No, no, no."

"Your mother gave you a book."

"No; I could not read."

"She sat you in front of educational television."

"No; it never meant anything to me."

I breathed; I drank; I ate; and after learning to crawl, I started to walk and then to run. Here I am many years later, and except for the clothes, everything came from that little foot of flesh and blood.

Many Christians think that by belonging to a company of believers, instantly they are made overcomers; instantly they are made full-grown saints.

"Where do you go?"

"I go to such and such a place. They have depth and good knowledge there because they know the Bible. They have such a great history."

But you gain nothing. In fact, when you have to give an account to the Lord, He will say, "Where were you?"

You will say, "Oh, I was in such and such a place, Lord."

"Then why did you not grow? How could you be in such a company and not grow?"

You just sat in a chair or a pew. You warmed it nicely for an hour, but that is all you ever did. While you sat there, you thought of the meal that you were going to have later. Or you sat there, thinking, "I must buy those stocks first thing in the morning. This is the solution to the problem in my business."

You cannot hide in other people's experience and faith. Even if you knew brother Watchman Nee, you could not hide in his experience. You have to have your own experience; you have to grow yourself; you have to gain the victory in your circumstances. You are the one who has to make decisions on principle. Then you grow.

There are only three materials out of which the bride is made and the capital city is produced—gold, precious stones, pearl. All three of these materials are exceedingly precious, and they all speak of the life and character of the Lord Jesus. All three mean that we have one single life. Normally, this life is seventy years, but we do not know how long it will be. But in that one single life, we have to be saved and filled with the Holy Spirit, lay down our life and be changed into the image of the Lord Jesus. We have to learn to walk with the Lord and keep in first love. In this one little life, this gold of the Lord Jesus has to be discovered by us and be purged and purified in us. It has to become us, and then it goes into the city. This precious stone has to be discovered, mined, cut, polished, created into something of unbelievable beauty—and all in this one little life. In one short life, a bit of grit has to be formed into a pearl as it gets coated over and over again.

Many Christians have the idea that this gold is already fashioned and beautiful, and the Lord has it all ready. "Come," He says, "the gold, the precious stone, and the pearl are all ready." It is not like that.

We have to find the gold, and it is often where we least expect it. In Genesis 2 we have to follow the river to find gold. It is in the land of Havilah, which in Hebrew means "sand." If we go to the sandy place, we find the gold buried in the river bed, and it has to be sieved. Then it has to be melted and purified.

In following the river, we will find onyx stone, which was the stone on the shoulders of the high priest. There were twelve precious stones on his breast, one for each tribe, but on his shoulders, all twelve were summed up in one precious stone. Where do you find this precious stone? It is hidden in the dark.

If I had a huge sapphire in its rough, uncut state, it would be enough to keep you the whole of your life. But as you look at it, you would probably say, "What has he got that rock for? Don't bring that dirty looking thing in the house; it looks worthless." I could even have a big diamond, and you would hardly even recognize it as a diamond. However, buried in your problems, in your circumstances, and in the seeming catastrophes of your life, there are precious stones, and there is gold.

Suppose I brought a little bit of worthless grit and said to you: "See this bit of grit. Does anybody want it?" You would all say that you had plenty of that in the back yard and you did not need it. Do you know that at the heart of every genuine pearl there is a worthless bit of grit? Sometimes, a problem comes into your life or a sickness, and you ask the Lord to take it away. But the Lord says, "My grace is sufficient." Then a coat goes over the grit, and another, and another, until a pearl is produced.

We all want to go to great meetings, and in these meetings, we hope we might obtain gold, precious stone and pearl. We want to have a tremendous spiritual experience which will mean that, suddenly, the Lord will give us gold, precious stone, or pearl in its finished state. No; it is not so! You have only one single life, and in this life, you will find the gold in its rough state; it is the gold of Christ. You will find the precious stone in its rough state; it is the character of the Lord Jesus. You will find the pearl— no, you will find the grit, and God will make the pearl in your one short life.

Generally, I tell people something like this. When I was young, birthdays used to be a millennium away. When I was three or four years of age, I would go to my mother and say, "When is my next birthday?" My mother would say, "You just had your birthday." But I would say, "When is my next birthday?" She would say, "In a year's time." Then I knew I would have to wait, and it seemed to me that it was forever and ever. To me, the Lord could have created the whole universe and four or five more in the time between one birthday and the next. I looked on birthdays as a time when I was given presents. I judged every one of my relatives by the kind of presents they gave, and I did not think much of those who gave me clothing. I wanted something else for my birthday. Then, my next birthday would come, and then another millennium, and then another birthday, and then another millennium. It is not like that now. One after the other the birthdays come and go so fast. What has happened? The world must be spinning faster. How come it used to be so slow and now it is so fast?

We are all tomorrow people. "Tomorrow, I will get right with the Lord. Tomorrow, I will give the Lord first place in my home. Tomorrow, I will make the Lord first in my business life. I am too young; I need to have a little experience of this world—tomorrow." Then you get married, and you have all the problems of marriage. So you say, "Wait until I am a little older." Then when you are a little older, you have the middle-age spread, and you cannot be bothered. You become cynical and these words come forth: "I have seen it all." Then you think: "When I am retired, I will give myself wholly to the Lord." However, when you retire, you cannot hear and you cannot see. How clever the enemy is! Tomorrow—always tomorrow. But tomorrow never comes. God says, "Today! Today, if you will hear My voice, harden not your heart."

This is a priority—and it is you. God's priority is that you grow up to be full-grown. Are you willing to allow Him to be first in all things so that you may be presented perfect in Christ?

Israel

The last priority is Israel, and this is perhaps quite unbelievable. In Luke 2 we learn of a godly old man, Simeon. The Holy Spirit had revealed to him that he would not die until he actually saw the Messiah with his eyes. On this amazing occasion, he came into the temple, and he saw a little baby in the arms of a very young woman with an older man. Instantly, he knew in his heart: "This is the Messiah." As he took up the little baby, he said, "Now, Lord, let Your servant depart in peace, for my eyes have seen Your salvation which You have prepared before the face of all peoples, a light to lighten the Gentiles, and the glory of Your people Israel" (see Luke 2:29–32).

I have no doubt that Simeon was a godly man and that God had shown him many things. Clearly, he had an understanding of the central position the Messiah was to occupy. He had spent much time meditating and pondering on the Scriptures in the Old Testament. So why did he say "The salvation which You have prepared before the face of all peoples, a light to lighten the Gentiles (first), and (then) the glory of Your people Israel"?

If we follow the normal Christian theology, Jesus, who was born Jewish, came to the Jews. It says so in Romans 9:5: "Of whom also is the Messiah according to the flesh, who is God blessed for ever." Why didn't Simeon say, "This salvation which You prepared before the face of all peoples is the glory of Your people Israel and

Four Priorities on the Heart of God   53

the light to lighten the Gentiles;" that is, the Messiah first came to the Jews? The Lord Jesus Himself was to say, "Salvation is of the Jews." So why did he not understand that first the early church would be all Jewish? It was. All the twelve apostles were not half Jewish, not a quarter Jewish, but they were fully Jewish. All the early church leaders, with those great Greek names—Stephen, Philip, Apollos, Barnabas, Timothy—were all Jewish. Why did he not say, "Yeshua is the glory of Your people Israel"? Instead, he said, "A light to lighten the Gentiles,"—as if the major work in this age would be among non-Jews—"and the glory of Your people Israel." Jesus has never been the glory of the Jewish people. He has been from God's standpoint, but not from the Jewish people's standpoint.

Then He said something else interesting: "This child is set for the falling and rising of many in Israel"—as if the fall would come first, and the rising would come last. Do you recall that in the early church there was an enormous controversy? It had to do with the Gentiles being saved and what to do with the Gentiles. Should we make them Jews? Should they observe the whole law of Moses? Should they be circumcised? There were many in the early church who said they must conform to Jewish Law. So there was an enormous argument. Should the Gentiles who come to the Lord "keep kosher?" In other words, should they keep kosher Law? It was not just a question of legalism; it was a question of quality. That was what the huge problem was with the early church, because with kosher Law, there was quality. "We can have them for a meal to have fellowship with us, but what do we do if they ask us back? We do not know what they are cooking in their kitchen." This was a big problem.

Then all the leaders of the church came together for a big conference, and this is how it ended: "And after they had held their peace, James answered, saying, Brethren, hearken unto me: Simeon hath rehearsed how first God visited the Gentiles, to take out of them a people for his name. And to this agree the words of the prophets; as it is written, After these things I will return, and I will build again the tabernacle of David, which is fallen" (Acts 15:13–16a).

Why did James use the little word first? No one has ever adequately explained that to me. Why did he say, "Simeon (that is, Peter) hath rehearsed how first God visited the Gentiles"? Should he not have said, "How God first visited the Jews to take out a people for His name, and now He has saved the Gentiles"? But he did not say that. He said, "Simeon, the apostle Peter, has told us how God first has begun this work among the Gentiles, and with this agrees the prophet. After these things, I will build up the tabernacle of David, which is fallen."

What I am trying to say is that God's major focus in the whole of this age or dispensation has been the Gentiles. It is true that the gospel was first preached to the Jew and then the Greek. It is true that the early church was a remnant of Israel that was saved. But then, the main focus of the work of the Holy Spirit has been unto all the nations, beginning in Jerusalem, going into Judea, into Samaria, and to the uttermost parts of the earth. But it is a fallacy when Christians believe that God has finished with the Jewish people.

"For if thou wast cut out of that which is by nature a wild olive tree, and wast grafted contrary to nature into a good olive tree; how much more shall these, which are the natural branches, be grafted into their own olive tree? For I would not, brethren, have you ignorant of this mystery, lest ye be wise in your own conceits, that a hardening in part hath befallen Israel, until the fulness of the Gentiles be come in; and so all Israel shall be saved" (Romans 11:24–26a).

"As touching the gospel, they are enemies for your sake: but as touching the election, they are beloved for the fathers' sake. For the gifts and the calling of God are irrevocable" (Romans 11:28–29).

The focal point of the Holy Spirit's work in this age has been to call out from the Gentiles a people for His name. But as that work draws to its completion, God will turn again to the Jewish people, and He will touch their blindness and the hardening, and He will save them. You are the witnesses of the recreation of Israel—the fig tree back in its original soil. This is evidence that we are in those days.

Do you believe that God has worked all these miracles in the Middle East only for the physical? Do you believe that He has recreated the fertility out of desert, swamp land, and eroded hills, only for fertility? Do you believe He has brought back physically the Jews from ninety-two different nations after nineteen hundred years of exile, and that is all? Do you believe that the cities which have been ruined for two thousand years have been rebuilt in our day and generation? If you study the prophets, you will see that this is the precise fulfillment in a detailed manner of the prophecy of the prophets. Do you believe that Hebrew, which ceased to be spoken as a spoken language for seventeen hundred years, has been reborn as a living language, and that is all? Do you believe that Israel has been preserved in six wars in forty-seven years, and more to come, and that is all? Do you believe that God is only interested in these physical miracles? If so, you have misread the heart of God.

The Last Chapter of the Love Story

The history of the Jewish people is a love story. It began with Abraham, and God has never fallen out of love with His people. You are in this love story. I am the physical seed of Abraham, and you are the spiritual seed of Abraham. He is the father of all who believe.

God's purpose for the church cannot be fulfilled without the Jewish people. We are in the last chapter of the love story, almost the last paragraph. May our eyes be opened to see it. May we live to see the greatest miracle of all—the salvation of the Jewish people. This will be the last bit of evidence that God will set before the nations, when the Jewish people will turn to the Lord Jesus and recognize Him, and He will become the glory of God's people, Israel. Do you understand that this is a priority? It was not a priority before this century, but now it is a priority. There is no way the people of God can walk with the Lord and not recognize this priority.

God is going to shake this world to pieces. He so loves this Jewish people that He turned the Kremlin upside down because they would not let the Jewish people go home. One million have come home, and another million have visas.

We have only to see a Zhirinovsky or some other violently anti-Semitic human come to power, and they will all come. That will be the end of the so-called peace process. Yes, there are more wars to come, more troubles and sufferings for the Jewish people, but it will end in their salvation, for the Lord has set His love upon them and will not be outwitted.

The Fig Tree and the Last Days
How do we know we are in the last days? The Lord Jesus gave a great deal of signs. So how are we to understand these signs that the Lord Jesus gave us? He summed up this major discourse of His in one sentence: "From the fig tree, learn its parable." In other words, there is something specific, something particular about the fig tree. The other signs are general signs, but the fig tree is the specific sign. The other signs are invalid when the fig tree is not present. But once the sign of the fig tree is present and the other signs are present, then we know we have passed into the last phase of world history. I hope I have been able to give you solid evidence that the fig tree is Israel. The fig tree was to disappear from its natural habitat, and it would seem as if there had never been a fig tree there, But Jesus said that before He returns, the fig tree will be back in its original habitat—not as an antique, not as a fossil, not merely as an illustration, but as a living tree.

There is one thing about little Israel: she is not dead. Everybody has heard about Israel. The whole world discusses little Israel, with only six million people, in a tiny postage stamp of territory. It is no bigger than the state of New Jersey, Tasmania, or the north island of New Zealand. It is a little smaller than the Kruger National Game park in South Africa, the size of Wales in the United Kingdom, Portugal or Hungary in Europe. It is so small, but the whole world knows that Israel is alive. She has suddenly occupied the center of the world's stage, exactly as Zechariah the prophet said she would. Three times, he said: "All the nations of the earth will be gathered together against Jerusalem." What in the world would the nations come against Jerusalem for? A hundred years ago, Jerusalem was nothing but a little village town with thirty-eight thousand inhabitants—unhygienic, flea-bitten, fly-blown, half-ruined, the capital of nothing, buried in the Judean hill country in the Syrian province of the Ottoman Empire.

Why would nations come against Jerusalem? There is no oil, gas, coal, natural resources, and very little water. Why would they come against this little postage stamp of territory? But today, everybody understands. There have been six wars in forty-seven years, and they have all been over Jerusalem. Suddenly, something has happened that has changed the whole scene. Seemingly, from the ashes, like the phoenix, she has risen from the dead and occupied the center of the world's stage. Now we understand the prophet Zechariah when he said that one day the Messiah's feet will again stand upon the mount of Olives, and from this we understand the fig tree is very much alive and back in its original territory. The sign is there, and at the same time, there have been two world wars that have shaken the whole world, and wars and rumors of war ever since.

Now we understand that the Lord is shaking everything according to the prophets Haggai and Zechariah and the writer of the Hebrew letter. God said He would shake all nations, and the desire of all nations shall come. The writer of the Hebrews said that everything that can be shaken, God is going to shake.

Receiving a Kingdom Unshakable

If the lives of the children of God consist very largely of the shakable, they will be shaken. If we are receiving a kingdom that cannot be shaken, if our lives are centered in the unshakable One, we will neither be shaken nor moved. But how much of the kingdom is in our lives? What place does the unshakable King of glory have in our lives? What place does He have in our families? What place does He have in our business life? What place does He have in our church life? If He has the place that God has given Him, we shall be unshakable, as invincible as the King, as immovable as the King. Jesus said, "Upon this rock, I will build My church; and the gates of hell shall not prevail against it." But if our heart is in the wrong place, then we are going to see a lot of shaking in our lives. We are going to lose a lot. We are going to be harmed. This is why this matter is so important.

Redeem the Time

The apostle Paul said, "Look therefore carefully how ye walk, not as unwise, but as wise; redeeming the time, because the days are evil" (Ephesians 5:15–16). In other words, our family life, personal life, business life, and our fellowship life can be a redeeming of the time; but if we are unwise, like the unwise virgins, we shall lose a lot. This word is not to unsaved people; it is to the child of God; it is to the church of God. "Wherefore be ye not foolish, but understand what the will of the Lord is." In every generation of the church, in every generation of the people of God, going back to Abraham, there have been foolish believers and there have been understanding believers. The understanding know what the will of God is for their generation. They are the wise, and, therefore, they put first things first. They give the Lord His place. They understand the priorities of God in their generation.

Some people say: "Are you saying that we should not be in business? Maybe we should not get married. Perhaps we should be like monks and nuns." No, I am not saying anything like that. If you need to get married, get married, but see to it that you give the Lord His place. Let your home and family be a place where God is known. Redeem the time. Of course, you can go into business. Make as much money as you can; but give the Lord His place. Do not let money rule you. Do not let success rule you. Give the Lord His place, and then your business will be redeeming the time.

Indeed, God has His heart set on these four priorities—the gospel, the bride, you, and Israel. He will shake everything to pieces in order to fulfill His heart's desire—but He will fulfill it. With His desire in view, what is our responsibility in these last days?

> Look therefore carefully how you walk, not as unwise,
> but as wise; redeeming the time, because the days
> are evil. Wherefore be ye not foolish, but understand
> what the will of the Lord is. Ephesians 5:15–17

Shall we pray:

Dear Lord, we just bow here in Your presence. We need You, Lord. We pray that somehow these priorities that are on Your heart in these last days may be on our hearts. Bring us into an identity of purpose with Yourself so that the burden of Your heart becomes the burden of our heart and Your purpose becomes our purpose. Dear Lord, deliver us from the shakable, deliver us from frittering away our whole lives by being centered in that which will pass away. Beloved Lord, by Your Spirit, work in our hearts, and we shall give You the praise and glory. We ask it in the name of the Lord Jesus. Amen.

Other books by Lance Lambert

The Uniqueness of Israel

Woven into the fabric of Jewish existence there is an undeniable uniqueness. There is bitter controversy over the subject of Israel, but time itself will establish the truth about this nation's place in God's plan. For Lance Lambert, the Lord Jesus is the key that unlocks Jewish history He is the key not only to their fall, but also to their restoration. For in spite of the fact that they rejected Him, He has not rejected them.

Till the Day Dawns

"And we have the word of prophecy made more sure; whereunto ye do well that ye take heed, as unto a lamp shining in a dark place, until the day dawn, and the day-star arise in your hearts." (II Peter 1:9).

The word of prophecy was not given that we might merely be comforted but that we would be prepared and made ready. Let us look into the Word of God together, searching out the prophecies, that the Day-Star arise in our hearts until the Day dawns.

Talks With Leaders

"O Timothy, guard that which is committed unto thee ..." (1 Timothy 6:20) Has God given you something? Has God deposited something in you? Is there something of Himself which He has given to you to contribute to the people of God? Guard it. Guard that vision which He has given you. Guard that understanding that He has so mercifully granted to you. Guard that experience which He has given that it does not evaporate or drain away or become a cause of pride. Guard that which the Lord has given to you by the Holy Spirit. In these heart-to-heart talks with leaders Lance Lambert covers such topics as the character of God's servants, the way to serve, the importance of anointing, and hearing God's voice. Let us consider together how to remain faithful with what has been entrusted to us.

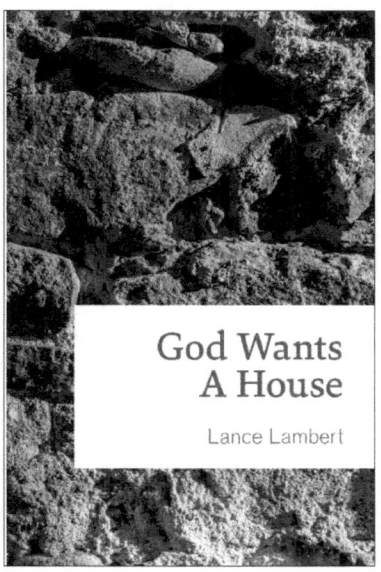

God Wants a House

Where is God at home? Is He at home in Richmond, VA? Is He at home in Washington? Is He at home in Richmond, Surrey? Is He at home in these other places? Where is God at home? There are thousands of living stones, many, many dear believers with real experience of the Lord, but where has the ark come home? Where are the staves being lengthened that God has finally come home? In God Wants a House Lance looks into this desire of the Lord, this desire He has to dwell with His people. What would this dwelling look like? Let's seek the Lord, that we can say with David, "One thing have I asked of Jehovah, that will I seek after: that I may dwell in the house of Jehovah all the days of my life, To behold the beauty of Jehovah, And to inquire in his temple."

www.ingramcontent.com/pod-product-compliance
Lightning Source LLC
Chambersburg PA
CBHW061343040426
42444CB00011B/3058